A start me up Book

Castles

By Hans-Peter von Peschke
Illustrated by Nikolay Smirnov

Book illumination, 1405.

Tessloff Publishing

Preface

Castles spark our imagination like no other building can. They are the setting for countless adventures in books, movies, and television. Castles are the scene of fierce battles in which knights try to storm the walls, but they are also the scene of great celebrations where armies of servants file into the Great Hall carrying silver trays piled high with magnificent foods.

These legends and adventures encourage us to associate castles with strange stories and dark secrets. We think of secret passageways and treasure chambers, dungeons and torture chambers, fair damsels and noble warriors. If you visit an actual castle, however, you'll probably start wondering about a lot of plain, everyday things. How were people back then able to build such massive walls without the help of technology like we have today? Did the siege tower really roll up the hill as easily as it seems in movies? How did a drawbridge actually work? Did the castle's residents take baths, was there any school, what kinds of games did children and adults play? And wasn't it extremely cold in a castle?

This book will answer some of these questions. A lot of recent research on the Middle Ages looks less at great battles and kings and more at the private lives of both commoners and nobles. This research has cleared away many of the romantic notions that obscured our understanding of life in a castle. Now that we understand life in the Middle Ages more accurately, castles may not make us think of adventures and mystery so much any more. Even so, there is a new kind of excitement in discovering what life in a castle was really like.

Volume 10

PUBLISHERS: Tessloff Publishing, Quadrillion Media LLC

EDITOR: Alan Swensen

PICTURE SOURCES:
Archiv fuer Kunst und Geschichte, Berlin: 1, 13, 19, 23, 29, 31, 32r, 35, 38, 41, 45, 46;
Bildarchiv Preussischer Kulturbesitz, Berlin: 11, 26, 27, 30, 32l, 44; Historic Scotland, Edinburgh: 8t;
ZEFA, Dusseldorf: 8b, 9;
COVER: Nikolay Smirnov
ILLUSTRATIONS: Nikolay Smirnov

Contents

How Castles Came About

A peasant brings news of enemy hordes that are devastating the countryside.

The following imaginary scene, set in the early Middle Ages, in a region exposed to enemies on all sides—Germany—illustrates some of the reasons for building castles.

> **Why were castles first built?**

Johann, Richard, and Heinrich were afraid. The peasant Johann looked terrified as he reported to the king: "They came without warning. They rode out of the forest on small, shaggy horses and raced toward our houses. Arrows were flying everywhere and some of them were burning and set the thatched roofs of our houses on fire. I managed to close the heavy wooden door and push the beam into place to lock it, but we didn't stand a chance. We tried to put out the fires as the arrows rained down on us, but they threw ropes around the logs in the palisade and used their horses to pull it down. They killed all of the men and boys, stole all of our belongings and supplies, and carried off our women. They only left me because they thought I was dead..."

Count Richard was doubly afraid. First, he was afraid of the enemy who for years now had repeatedly attacked the border region he was supposed to protect, and second, of his king, who looked at him now with disappointment in his eyes. "We don't stand a chance against these hordes, Sire! We can never get to the villages in time! We find out soon enough that there are Huns hiding in our forests—who could

MOST CASTLES were built during the 9th to the 16th centuries. These were times when Europe's noble families were constantly at war with each other. They built castles all over Europe and in the Near East. International wars like the Crusades encouraged the building of castles.

The villagers didn't stand a chance against the Huns and their fast horses.

miss the clouds of smoke and the raging fires they leave wherever they go?" he said, bitterly. "But they won't stand and fight us! By the time we march to the village being attacked, all we find are corpses and the smoking remains of houses. Sometimes a few villagers are able to hide or to play dead, like Johann here. We just aren't fast enough—we can't protect things here anymore. Everything we build up these miserable robbers destroy. God is punishing us, my Lord!"

Heinrich I, the king, was also afraid, but of course he couldn't let anyone see it. Maybe the end of the world really is near, like the priests say, he thought. And we are fighting against Satan's hordes on every side. In the South there are the fierce Saracens, and from the North, the godless Vikings sail up our rivers in their rapid boats and attack our villages, and then there are these Huns from the East. But it is now the year of Our Lord 923, and that means 77 more years

until the Last Judgment. If we are to stand at that day and attain our eternal salvation, every one of us must prove himself a good Christian here and now!

"It cannot go on like this," the king said—more to himself than to his liegemen. "We have to take action, but differently than we have so far. It won't do any good to march once more into the Steppes of the East—even with the greatest of armies. The Huns don't have any cities or any territories with clear boundaries where we could surround and capture them and their lands. I shall send messengers to the leaders of the Huns and offer them even more tribute and more gold than they could get by plundering our lands..."

Johann and Richard stand thunderstruck as they listen to their lord, who is smiling bitterly. "By doing this we will buy ourselves ten years of peace. During this time we will create our own army of mounted warriors. They will have better armor than these

robbers and murderers and will be nearly as fast—a real army of knights. Above all, however, we need to protect ourselves better against their raids. We must build fortified places throughout the kingdom, places that will be difficult to attack. From these places we can keep watch over the land. If the enemy attacks, the peasants can retreat into these fortified places with their families, animals, and supplies. Then, Johann, you will no longer lose your possessions, and you, Richard, will no longer arrive too late to help. Therefore, let us build castles!"

Even in the remote past humans

<table>
<tr><td>

Were there castles before the Middle Ages?

</td><td>

looked for sites that were difficult to find and to attack. Such sites might be remote valleys or

</td></tr>
</table>

other places that were protected on nearly all sides by cliffs, rivers, or lakes. The narrow road leading into the site was blocked by a wooden or stone wall so it could be defended by a small number of men, even against a much larger force. When danger threatened, humans retreated into such refuges with their possessions.

The great civilizations of the ancient world protected their villages and cities with walls of wood or stone. They tried to take advantage of natural protection provided by water or terrain.

Europeans learned from the Romans how to build fortified settlements. Roman fortifications consisted of a square "castellum" (Latin for "small fortified place") surrounded by an embankment and often several moats as well. This was designed to protect the legions from enemy attacks. Barracks, stalls, and storage buildings were surrounded on all sides by a high, thick wall. At each corner there was a huge watchtower.

Forerunners of the Castle

One predecessor of what we now call castles was the Roman *castellum*. In many European languages the terms for such buildings remind us of this connection: the English word "castle,"

the Italian word "castello," and even the French word "château" all come from the Latin word "castellum."

Another type of fortification, the "burgus," also influenced European castles. This was a four-sided watchtower surrounded by a strong wall of wooden stakes—a palisade—and a moat filled with water. The German word for castle ("Burg") and the ending in many English place names—Pittsburg—come from "burgus."

WARFARE

In the centuries before the Middle Ages, the "wild" peoples of Northern Europe often fought against each other, but when they had to fight the Romans they found their methods were inadequate. The well-trained, well-organized Romans were able to defeat much larger armies of fierce but poorly organized warriors. Enemies who came on horseback and attacked suddenly, without warning—like the Saracens, the Vikings, and the Huns—could only be defeated by well-trained, mobile troops of professional soldiers.

first line of defense in the lower village, and peasants from the surrounding area fled into the lower village with their animals and provisions. They didn't retreat into the upper castle unless it looked like the lower village was going to fall into enemy hands. During the time of the Vikings, thousands of these mottes were built. Centuries later some of these early fortifications could still be found alongside actual castles.

These fortifications had one major weakness: they were made of wood. The wall couldn't withstand battering rams or catapults and, above all, they caught fire easily. This is why some rulers soon began building the lower part of the walls—and later the entire building—out of stone. In the meantime many of the builders gave up the practice of making an artificial hill and simply dug a large trench or moat around the site.

The forerunner of later castles was the so-called "motte," a wooden tower built on an artificial hill and surrounded by a palisade. At the base of the motte there was often a palisaded village.

PROFESSIONAL KNIGHTS

In reaction to the new kind of warfare—fierce warriors attacking suddenly on horseback—kings, dukes, and other rulers created attack troops consisting primarily of knights. These were heavily armed, mounted soldiers— far superior to foot soldiers.

What were the first castles like?

The first castles were built of wood and didn't really look very strong. The most common kind was the "motte." This was a large, man-made dirt mound with a two- or three-story tower on top. It was usually surrounded by a palisade. In most cases a kind of fortified village grew up around the base of the motte, and it was also protected by a log palisade and connected to the upper castle by a stairway. Sometimes both the hill and the village were further protected by a man-made moat surrounding the whole complex.

If an enemy threatened to attack, the inhabitants set up their

How did builders choose a site?

Since castles were built above all to offer protection from attackers, the builders looked for a site with as much natural protection as possible. A source of water was also of vital importance. A deep well that didn't dry up even in times of drought and that couldn't be reached from any other place was absolutely necessary if the castle was to withstand a siege. The castle also needed to be fairly near to the farmsteads of the ruler's subjects, and to trade routes. After all, the lord of the castle wanted to rule his entire territory, his "fief," from this castle.

What kinds of castles were there?

The favorite building sites for castles were hill or mountain tops with steep slopes on all sides and a good view out over the surrounding country. The advantages of building a castle on a high spot were clear. It was very difficult for attackers to get battering rams or siege towers up to the castle—if they could get them up at all. It was also easy for castle dwellers to throw rocks or shoot flaming arrows down onto the attackers from the castle walls. One problem, however, was getting building materials to the site. Workers often had to construct complicated bridges to make access to the site possible. In times of peace these bridges made it easier for horses and wagons to reach the castle.

A builder could avoid this disadvantage by finding a site that had natural protection on three sides

Caerlaverock Castle in Scotland is unique for its triangular form. Built around 1280, it had strong towers at each corner and a double moat.

and convenient access on the fourth. This was the case on a ridge jutting out from a mountain or land jutting out into the sea, for example, or at a tight bend in a river. Strong walls and an especially massive and well-fortified gateway protected the side of the castle open to the surrounding area.

The terrain didn't always offer such ideal sites, however. In the plains of Northern Europe, for example, castles had thicker walls and deeper moats than in mountainous areas. Often the builder had an artificial hill constructed and channeled water from a nearby river or lake into a surrounding moat. These castles did have one important advantage over those

FEUDALISM, the social order during the Middle Ages, was a system in which powerful rulers ("liege lords") granted lands to their less powerful subjects. Kings granted lands to dukes, and dukes granted lands to counts or knights. With the lands they also received the right to rule over all the people living there. In exchange for these lands the "liegemen" had to provide troops for the liege lord when he went to war. They were also expected to protect their fief against invaders. In later centuries knights could buy their way out of this obligation to fight for the liege lord. The lord then used this money to pay for professional soldiers.

Chillon Castle in Switzerland is built on an island in Lake Geneva. Its only connection with the mainland was by drawbridge.

NOBILITY AND CLERGY

The feudal system was organized like a pyramid. At the top were the nobles—the first "estate." They bore arms and defended their land. The second estate was the clergy (priests, monks, etc.) with the pope at its head. They prayed for the well-being of their land, provided religious education, and cared for the poor.

THE THIRD ESTATE formed the base of the pyramid. It was made up of peasants and tradesmen. Many of the members of this estate—it included more than 80 percent of the population—were practically enslaved and had no rights. Without their lord's permission they weren't allowed to marry or to move to another place.

The social pyramid was divided into three levels: nobility, clergy, and peasantry.

with greater natural protection: they were close to the fields and pastures of the peasants.

In addition to these basic types of castles there were many more variants. There were castles built at the openings of caves. They were chiseled into the side of a mountain around an already exist-

The design of a castle was often determined by the terrain where it was built. The Wartburg in Thuringia, Germany was built on a steep hill and was difficult to attack.

ing cave. There were also castles built on natural or artificial islands in a river or lake.

Over time castles became the administrative center where the lord or his representative collected taxes and goods paid by the peasants as rent for their land. Castles were also where court was held and where public punishments were executed. There were also scribes at the castle who

Were castles just for protection?

recorded and sealed contracts and treaties.

In addition, the castle was the home of the castle lord and his family and was made as comfortable as possible. For the higher nobility it became more and more important to have a castle that was not only secure but also impressive. The more splendid the castle, the greater the prestige of the owner among his peers! Apparently the height of the castle made a particularly strong impression, since later castle builders tried to outdo each other with taller and taller structures. Powerful rulers such as dukes or counts might own several castles and this was a reflection of their wealth and power. Emperors and kings had palaces (from Latin *palatium*) in many cities. These palaces had very ornate rooms and also a throne room where the emperor or king would "hold audience"—a kind of "office hour" when people could come and speak with him. These early palaces were basically fortified city homes, but later rulers had more massive structures built—like the imperial castle in Nuremberg, Germany. It was built to control an important trade route that ran through the area. Later, however, it was mostly used as a representative building where the ruler could receive important guests and host important state events.

Building a Castle

Once the future lord of the castle had selected the best site for his new home, he couldn't just start building. He first had to get the consent of his "liege lord." Kings and other powerful rulers had learned through bitter experience that castles allowed people to resist not only Huns, Saracens, and Vikings, but also their own kings. They only allowed one of their

Who could build a castle?

vassals to build a castle if they were sure they could trust the vassal, and if the vassal had a good reason for building one. Such reasons included the protection of border areas, important trade roads, river crossings, monasteries, or cities.

Noblemen who neglected to ask for permission had to fear that the king's troops would come and demolish the "illegally" built castle. Toward the end of the Middle Ages, however, more and more

COMPULSORY LABOR

Not only did peasants have to give the feudal lord a share of their own harvest, they also had to work for him on his own estate—without pay. Peasants had to help their lord harvest hay in early summer and grain in late summer or early fall. When the lord built a castle, the amount of compulsory labor became even greater— much greater.

Stones and timbers were prepared at the building site or in the workshop and then dragged or carried up ramps. There were cranes on the walls that could raise lighter building materials up to the workers.

THE PEASANTS' ANIMALS

were also involved in compulsory labor agreements. One or two days a week the peasant had to work for his feudal lord and he was often required to bring his team of oxen or horses as well. On such work days, however, it was customary that the lord provide his "vassals" (the peasants he had granted land to) a good meal and occasionally some flour or porridge to take home.

AT THE BUILDING SITE

there was always a wooden shed, usually consisting of three walls and one open side. This was the stone masons' or carpenters' "lodge" where they could work when the weather was bad, and where they could store their tools. Since the same group of masons or carpenters usually worked together, the "lodge" soon came to stand for the people who worked in it. They also developed their own style in most cases, and the castles they built showed great similarities.

This medieval miniature shows a castle being built. In the lower left-hand corner is the workshop or lodge.

noblemen began to see their "fief"—the land assigned to their family centuries earlier by a liege lord who expected them to protect it for him—as their own property where they could build without needing anyone's permission. It wasn't uncommon for the liege lord to give them permission after the fact.

If the liege lord gave his permission for the construction of a castle, he also gave the builder the right to force the people living in the area where the castle was to be built to work for him. In exchange, these people then had the right to seek protection in the castle in times of war.

First the castle lord hired a mas-

> **Who designed the castle and what did the plans look like?**

ter builder who was responsible for planning the castle and overseeing its construction. This was an experienced builder and engineer. He would have gone through a long

apprenticeship as a stonecutter or mason on several big projects, and then worked with a church or castle builder who gave him a more thorough training. The reputation of such skilled craftsmen spread by word of mouth among the nobles.

After they agreed on a tidy sum of gold, the future lord of the castle and his master builder discussed what the castle should look like. It was usually modeled after a castle the nobleman had seen and found particularly impressive. The master builder proposed modifications that would make the castle even better. He also reached an agreement with his employer on the number and kinds of rooms to include in the castle, and on the number and kinds of auxiliary buildings around the castle. Then he calculated the number of workers needed and the kinds and amounts of materials required to build the castle. To pay the high costs, the lord might have to raise the rents and taxes he imposed on his subjects or even sell some of his property or go into debt.

There was no actual blueprint such as modern architects draw. The master builder may have scratched a simple sketch in wood or in the ground. Before construction began he marked out the basic outline of the building with stakes and string. For the most difficult parts of the building—the chapel's vaulted ceiling, for example—he made detailed drawings. Otherwise he relied on experience as his only guide. Since he had the plan in his head and there were no paper copies, he couldn't be fired. It was a catastrophe if he died before the building was finished.

It took several years to build a castle. These years were hard ones for the peasants living in the surrounding area, since

Who helped build the castle?

they had to work on the castle without pay. The lord of the castle authorized the master builder to put them to work wherever non-specialized workers were needed. This included breaking out rough blocks of stone at the quarry, cutting trees for timber, and clearing the building site. With their teams of oxen they had to deliver lumber, stone, sand, and lime. During the actual construction they assisted the craftsmen.

The craftsmen working on the project included quarrymen and masons, carpenters and roofers, blacksmiths and plumbers, and others. In addition to free room and board they received a good wage. After they completed the project, most of them moved on to a new building project. Some of them, however, stayed at the castle and helped maintain the castle and its surrounding facilities.

The castle walls were often more than 6 feet thick at the base. Some-

How did they raise the walls and towers?

times the walls at the base of a tower were even twice this thick. Towards the top the walls became thinner, however, since battering rams couldn't reach this high. First, using hammer and chisel, apprentices cut rough blocks from the larger pieces of stone. Then the journeymen and

IN SWAMPY AREAS

the workers drove pointed beams or posts many feet into the ground to create a solid foundation for walls and towers. They then laid crossbeams down on this foundation.

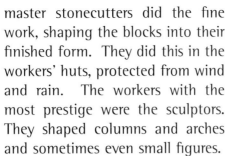

Workers load building materials onto sleds and then push the sleds up a spiral-shaped ramp that encircles the tower.

master stonecutters did the fine work, shaping the blocks into their finished form. They did this in the workers' huts, protected from wind and rain. The workers with the most prestige were the sculptors. They shaped columns and arches and sometimes even small figures.

To make the walls as strong as possible workers bound them together with mortar. Mortar is made of water, sand, and some kind of cement. To make cement the workers crushed limestone, burned it in an oven, and then ground it into powder. Every master mason had his own secret recipe for mortar. It sometimes included strange ingredients like coal dust, wine, or even buttermilk.

A wall consisted of three layers. On the inside and outside workers fit square stone blocks together with mortar. They filled the space between the inside and outside layers with rubble, crushed rock, and mortar.

Towers were an important part of the defensive system and were made especially strong. Each tower had three stories, which were connected by a spiral staircase attached to the inside of the tower wall.

Once the walls and towers rose above the heads of the workers, carpenters built scaffolding. This was made of logs tied firmly together with rope. The masons left holes in the outside layer of the wall—called putlog holes—and the carpenters pounded beams into these holes and fastened the

How did they build the battlements?

scaffolding to the beams. On a tower, the beams were spaced about six feet apart and each one was placed about two feet higher than the last. The carpenters then nailed planks on top of the beams and the result was a ramp that spiraled gently upward around the

This book "illumination" or illustration shows a besieged castle with attackers and defenders.

outside of the tower. Workers used this ramp to carry stones, mortar, and other building materials up to the masons. Sometimes they even used sleds pulled by rope to draw large stones up the ramp. In many of the castles remaining today you can still see the putlog holes where beams were placed for scaffolding.

Once the walls reached the desired height, masons built a small battlement—a wall to protect the soldiers as they fought off the enemy. Usually there were alternating high and low parts. In the higher parts there were often narrow slits ("arrow loops") through which the archers could shoot their arrows without exposing themselves to enemy arrows. Through the spaces in between—the lower parts of the battlement—the soldiers could throw rocks or other materials down onto the attackers.

While the masons were raising the walls, the master builder decided on the height of each story in the towers and taller buildings.

What supported the upper floors?

The heavy beams that supported the crossbeams for the ceiling were set into holes in the wall or they were rested on ledges the masons built into the walls. This wasn't strong enough for very large rooms, however. In these cases the carpenters built massive wooden columns under the beams so they wouldn't break even under heavy loads. Each individual piece of wood was cut to size in a workshop at the building site. The craftsmen laid the beams and planks down and fitted them together tightly. They then bored holes in the beams and planks so that they could pound in the wooden pegs that held the pieces together. They usually made the pegs from the unusually hard wood at the core of an oak tree.

In the earliest times the roofs of castles were covered with the same material as peasants' homes were: bundles of reeds, straw, or ferns.

How did they build the roof?

A roof like this was very flammable, however. The builder pitched the roof toward the inner

This cross section of a tower shows what the inside looked like. The lowest level was used as a storage room. The upper rooms were used either as guard rooms for the soldiers or for living quarters for the lord and his family.

courtyard so that it wasn't so easy to hit it with a burning arrow.

In the later part of the Middle Ages most castle lords preferred tile roofs. Those who had enough money and very strong roof trusses even used plates of lead to cover the roof. They were cast in sand forms and then fused together. The same craftsman who made the lead plates for the roof also manufactured the lead pipes that channeled rainwater into specially

HEAVY LOADS such as stones and logs were brought to the building site in oxcarts. Later they started using horses as well. At the actual building site workers transported mortar and rubble in baskets carried on their backs. For heavier loads they used stretchers and later wheelbarrows.

CRANES were also used at the building site. On the end of a horizontal beam there was a wheel or pulley that supported a rope. At first workers pulled the rope by hand—perhaps using a winch—to raise the materials at the other end. Later they developed a drive wheel that worked something like the wheel in a hamster cage: two men walked inside the wheel and the wheel reeled in the rope.

THE SIMPLE TOOLS used by the craftsmen weren't all that different from some we still use today. Digging was done with a pickaxe (1) and shovel. Stone masons needed hammers and chisels above all, but also mortar mixing hoes and trowels. Carpenters used axes, and pit or frame saws (2). They also used various drills and augers (3). The master builder's tools included a measuring cord and a plumb line (4), wooden squares (5), and a compass (6).

prepared storage tanks called "cisterns."

Smaller buildings inside the castle walls were built in "half-timber" style. Carpenters made a wooden frame out of vertical and horizontal wooden beams. In the spaces created by this grid they wove a mesh of pliable willow branches. The mason's assistants then mixed clay, straw, animal hair, and dung and filled in the areas between the beams with this material and smoothed out the surface. When it dried they whitewashed the surface.

Building vaulted ceilings was especially difficult and generally used only in the castle chapel. First the carpenters built a framework to support the stones as they were set one on top of the next. In the middle of the arch they fit the keystone, which was so precisely shaped that it fit almost seamlessly. Once the keystone was in place the vault could stand alone, and the workers removed the framework.

The buildings in the castle ward were usually simple half-timber structures. The roof was usually made of slate.

The castle residents needed water for drinking, cooking, washing, and also for hosing down stables and in general for washing away filth. Almost all castles had a deep well in the basement level. It was fed by a subterranean spring that didn't dry out during dry seasons. Since it was under the castle it couldn't be poisoned or blocked by enemies. The water was drawn up in wooden buckets on the end of long ropes.

> **How did they get water to the castle?**

Sometimes the well—essential to life in the castle—stood in the middle of the inner ward. In such cases it was enclosed in a wooden house so animal droppings or other filth wouldn't pollute the water.

Many castles had large cisterns in the attic level. Lead-lined gutters channeled rainwater into these cisterns. Water was piped from these containers into the various floors of the castle below. Such "running" water was a great luxury, however.

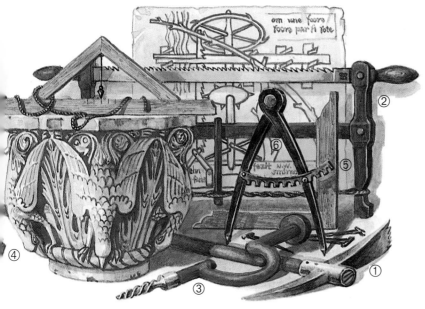

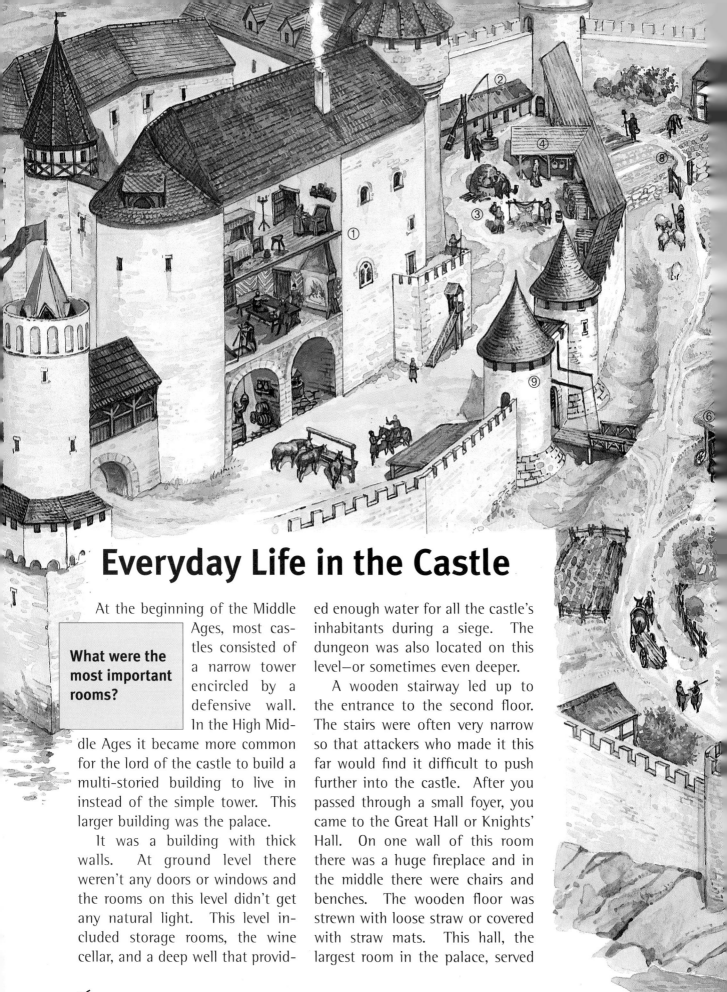

Everyday Life in the Castle

What were the most important rooms?

At the beginning of the Middle Ages, most castles consisted of a narrow tower encircled by a defensive wall. In the High Middle Ages it became more common for the lord of the castle to build a multi-storied building to live in instead of the simple tower. This larger building was the palace.

It was a building with thick walls. At ground level there weren't any doors or windows and the rooms on this level didn't get any natural light. This level included storage rooms, the wine cellar, and a deep well that provid-

ed enough water for all the castle's inhabitants during a siege. The dungeon was also located on this level—or sometimes even deeper.

A wooden stairway led up to the entrance to the second floor. The stairs were often very narrow so that attackers who made it this far would find it difficult to push further into the castle. After you passed through a small foyer, you came to the Great Hall or Knights' Hall. On one wall of this room there was a huge fireplace and in the middle there were chairs and benches. The wooden floor was strewn with loose straw or covered with straw mats. This hall, the largest room in the palace, served both as a place for the lord to receive guests and as a dining hall for guests and castle inhabitants.

In the old towers people usually had to use a wooden ladder to get from one floor to the next, but in the palace there was often a spiral staircase that led to the upper and lower levels. In one corner of the floor there was usually a trap door and a wooden

In the center of the castle complex was the palace (1), the residence of the castle lord. It generally included living quarters and a large dining and reception hall. The well (2), the bake oven (3), and the kitchen (4) were usually inside the inner curtain or wall. Stables (5), blacksmith's shop and other workshops (6) were located in the outer ward, as were the servants' houses (7) and castle garden (8). Like the inner ward's gate (9), with its drawbridge and portcullis, the gate leading into the outer ward was also protected by a strong gatehouse, water-filled moats, and a wall (10).

framework above it with a roll of rope and a winch. With this device servants could haul heavy objects up to the upper floors.

The living and sleeping areas of the lord's family were located in one or more floors above the main hall. Often the castle had only one room with a fireplace and this became the living and sleeping quarters. Sometimes, however, there might be an entire wing that had several heated rooms, and below them there might be a chapel, the lord's armory, or a room where servants spun, sewed, and embroidered.

The palace was a small fortress in itself, but it was also encircled by a defensive wall. There was very little room in the castle ward for other buildings, and the few that were built nestled up against the wall of the ward. In larger castle complexes this core was surrounded by a second area—the outer ward—that was enclosed by another set of walls and gatehouses. Here there were many buildings.

What other buildings did the castle include?

The most important auxiliary building was the kitchen. Builders didn't like to see this structure too close to the palace, since the open hearths were a serious fire hazard. Whenever possible, the kitchen was built up against the ward wall in a building of its own. To keep food from getting cold or wet on its way to the palace, workers built a covered walkway between the kitchen and the palace. Next to the kitchen there was often a washing area and a bake oven. It wasn't very far to a well either.

Servants' houses—if there were any—were usually built up against the walls of the outer ward. The workshops of the blacksmiths, carpenters, and stone masons were also located here. In one corner of the inner ward there was usually a kitchen garden. Sometimes there were a few fruit trees or even a fish pond. The horse stables were also built along the walls of the castle, as were the dovecote and a cage for the falcons used in hunting.

What sort of people lived in a castle?

A middle-sized castle with a palace surrounded by a wall or "curtain" had about 60 to 80 inhabitants. Of this number a good dozen or so belonged to the family of the lord of the castle. Most of these family members were children or unmarried relatives. In addition there were about 10 hired soldiers who stood watch on the walls and regularly practiced using and maintaining their weaponry. They also helped the masons when the

THE LADY OF THE CASTLE was particularly important in the early Middle Ages. When the lord was away fighting a war or on a crusade, it was her job to run the castle with a firm hand. This included supervising the peasants and frequently even defending the castle and their possessions against enemies. There were also social duties such as caring for the sick and the poor.

THE THREAT OF FIRE

constantly plagued castle dwellers. Once a fire started it was nearly impossible to extinguish it since it was very hard to get enough water to the fire in time. Far more castles were destroyed by fire than by enemy attacks. One of the important duties of the night watch was to check all the rooms with fireplaces or stoves and make sure there were no glimmering coals left where they could start a fire.

Peasant women were subordinated to their husbands and had to work very hard.

In winter in particular, spinning and weaving were among the most important tasks of noblewomen. Many of the most valuable examples of medieval embroidery were made by noblewomen.

court clerks here. A master cook supervised the kitchen. The "equerry," the master of the castle lord's horses, managed the stables. In the outer ward the lord provided space for craftsmen. They made pots, leather goods, candles, and even weapons. The most powerful lords had a master huntsman who supervised the gamekeepers and hunting dogs.

castle walls needed repairs or when it was time to bring in the harvest. Sometimes they even helped the steward, who supervised the affairs of the castle, to collect taxes and other duties.

Laborers did the majority of the work in the fields, vineyards, and forests that belonged to the castle. Their wives served the lady of the castle as maidservants. Besides the manual laborers there were also several craftsmen. These included a stone mason and a carpenter who oversaw or took care of repairs. There was almost always something that needed repair. In addition to these two there was also a blacksmith, whose work consisted mainly of shoeing horses and repairing weapons. A castle chaplain also looked after the souls of the castle's residents. He usually served as priest for the surrounding villages as well.

In larger castle complexes hundreds of people bustled about. Besides a castle steward there were also scribes and

> **What were the duties of the lord and lady of the castle?**

You wouldn't know it from movies about knights, but a castle lord spent most of his time with peaceful activities associated with managing a large region. He was a mediator in disputes among his subjects, he pronounced judgment in legal cases, and set tax rates and quotas for forced labor. With the help of the castle chaplain or a scribe—knights usually couldn't write—he had documents drawn up—deeds, land grants, edicts, legal records, etc.

The lady of the castle managed the household. She oversaw supplies collected from the peasants and decided what had to be bought from the market or from traveling merchants to supplement these stores. She planned all meals, decided which animals to butcher and which foods to salt or dry or preserve in some other way.

The maidservants helped her prepare meals and tend the kitchen garden. In winter she also organized her maidservants and had them make fabrics and clothing.

Life in a castle wasn't nearly as romantic as it appears in books and movies. There were few fireplaces and these were not very effective at heating large stone rooms. On stormy days the wind whistled through the rooms. At night there was little or no light in the halls and staircases. Rats rustled around in the straw spread over the floors and kitchen smells mingled with the smells of filth.

What was it like living in a castle?

All of the castle's residents worked, even the lord's family. They worked from early in the morning until late in the day, and, with few exceptions, Sunday was the only day they had free. There was little leisure time and even less variety from day to day. Everyone looked forward to the lesser and greater celebrations that interrupted the monotony of everyday life.

Unlike people today, people living in castles didn't wash up every morning and evening. Water was much too precious for that. Still, most of them used a damp cloth to rinse off their bodies after a hard day of work and they also washed their hands—after all, they had to eat with them. They kept a bowl of water near the dining table for this purpose.

Did knights take baths?

Bathing was reserved for the castle lord's family—though others might take an occasional dip in a pond in summertime. Only his family could afford the luxury of heating water with scarce fire-

Vermin were one of the most serious plagues castle residents had to deal with. One of the housewife's regular duties was to comb lice from her husband's and children's hair.

wood. In later times a castle lord might even invite guests to bathe with him. His carpenters built a large tub for this, and lined the edges with fabric so no one would get a splinter from the tub.

Long, flowing hair was the pride of every wife and knights tended to grow beards and wear their hair in a medium-long "page" cut. Unfortunately for them, this created an ideal environment for lice to nest in, and lice were hard to get rid of once they settled in. Both men and women used fine combs several times a day to remove the lice and lice

Why did knights scratch so much?

DISEASES, hunger, and early death were a human's constant companions during the Middle Ages. If a person lived to be more than 40 years old it was considered to be an extraordinary gift from God. The castle residents fared somewhat better than the peasants did, but after a crop failure even they had to face a lean diet. In winter in particular their diet offered little variety. There were no fresh fruits or vegetables and they suffered from vitamin deficiencies as a result. Many people lost all their teeth at an early age.

INFANT MORTALITY RATES were very high. Babies were hit hardest by the poor hygienic conditions. Approximately half of all children died before the age of six. Even in castles the medieval saying rang true: "many children, many coffins!"

DOCTORS could only be found at the castles of the highest nobility. In all other cases the lady of the castle or one of her maidservants was responsible for taking care of the sick. She also served as midwife. The local priest or a monk tried to comfort the sick by praying for them, or, in the worst case, by performing the last rites.

eggs (nits) from their hair. Fleas were also sources of torment. Maidservants carefully held burning candles up to their master's and mistress' clothing to try to burn the vermin or at least drive them away. Since these techniques weren't very effective, castle residents frequently had to scratch the many itches caused by vermin.

When did castle residents get up?

Nature set the daily schedule of castle dwellers. The first chirping birds or crowing roosters awakened them, and the day lasted until it was too dark to work any more. People divided the day and night into twelve hours each. This meant that a daylight hour in summer was longer than one in winter. They didn't have a more precise way for measuring time, and it isn't likely anyone would have seen a need for one.

Only larger castles had watchmen who served as a kind of "alarm clock" by blowing a trumpet, or priests who marked time by ringing the bells for mass. For a long time only monks could tell time. At first they used large, thick candles with rings marked on them. When the candle burned down one ring, an hour had passed. Later there were water and sand clocks that worked in a similar way—when a certain amount had run out, an hour had passed.

Clocks like this ornate hourglass clock were more for decoration than for practical use. The divisions of the day were usually set according to sunrise and sunset.

Castle "garderobes" or toilets were usually located on the outside wall.

What about toilets?

Every floor of the castle had one or more bays projecting out from the face of the castle wall. These were the toilets or "garderobes." The seat was a stone slab with a round hole cut in the middle. Some of these garderobes even had several seats. In a few cases there were more comfortable seats made of wood, and sometimes even a wash basin.

The toilets for the lord's family were located next to the chimney shaft and were often nice and warm. The servants used straw or sponges to clean them.

The results of each "session" fell through a vertical shaft—either directly into the castle moat or into a "cesspit" at the bottom of the wall. This pit smelled terrible, of course. Since people in the Middle Ages believed that bad-smelling vapors made people sick, they were careful to have the cesspit and the moat cleaned out regularly.

Most of the castle's inside walls weren't plastered or painted. Only the chapel and the lord's living quarters were decorated—with a mural, perhaps, or a band of decorative carvings. Tapestries were luxurious wall coverings and a sign of great wealth. Glass was just as rare and was usually found only in the chapel's colored windows. Otherwise window openings were narrow and covered only with shutters. If a room did have glass windows, they were so valuable that the steward kept them locked up and only took them out when the lord or his guests were present.

How did they finish the walls and floors?

Occasionally the walls of one of the bedrooms were paneled with wood, and the floor was covered with tiles or a mosaic. Otherwise servants spread straw or chopped reeds on the wooden floors to make them softer and warmer. Since a lot of filth accumulated in this straw, however, it had to be changed every two weeks or so.

In most castles the interior spaces had little furniture or decoration. In the rooms on upper floors you could sit on benches in the window alcoves. In addition there were also three-

What were sleeping arrangements like?

WINDOWS were usually small and could be used as arrow loops during enemy attacks. All of the windows had wooden shutters that could be pulled shut, but only a few had glass. Glass was a luxury item. Toward the end of the Middle Ages bull's eye panes became popular. These small, round panes were thicker in the middle, and were made of impure, cloudy glass. These small, coarse panes weren't as expensive as smooth, large ones.

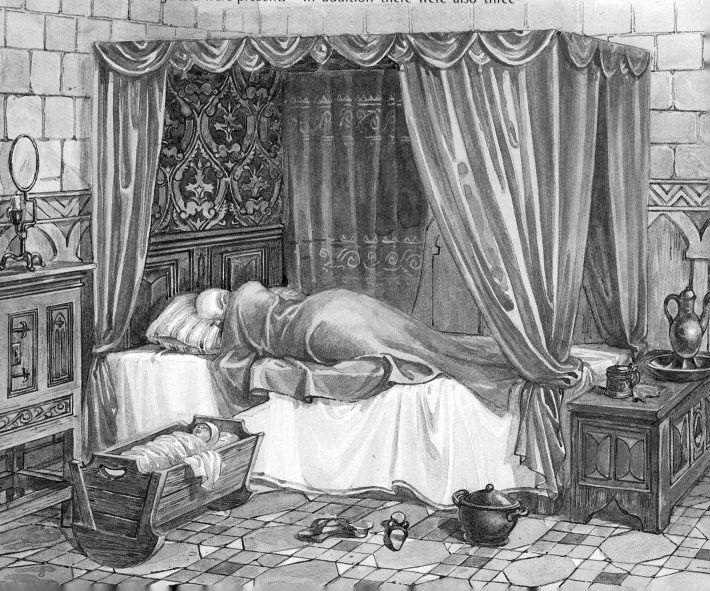

In the later part of the Middle Ages, windows were often made of bull's eye panes.

HEATING

Very few rooms in a castle had any heating. For this reason the household servants liked to sit around the kitchen hearth during winter months, and the lord and lady gathered their family and guests around the open fireplace in the Great Hall or in one of the private rooms that had a fireplace.

Private rooms were the first to get a tile stove instead of an open fireplace. The tile walls of the stove stored heat better than a fireplace could. There was also a bench built around the stove and this became a favorite gathering place in wintertime.

legged stools. Only in the Knight's Hall would you find a few carved chairs with high backs. They were meant for the lord and for his wife and their visitors. Everyone else sat on benches at long tables.

Wooden chests were used to store clothing. People put little bags of fragrant herbs like lavender in among the clothes to help protect them from moths. In the lord's bedchamber there were small cabinets that could be locked. He kept valuable possessions locked up here, but also food he could eat if he got hungry during the night.

The bed—if there was one—was the most important and most expensive piece of furniture. The mattress was usually stuffed with feathers or animal hair, though it might be no more than a bag of leaves or straw. Linen sheets were spread over the mattress. They changed them frequently since people didn't wear anything to bed. The blankets were also made of linen. On cold days they laid animal skins or bags of straw over the blankets. If they were very wealthy they might have expensive feather quilts.

A bed in those days had a tall frame that reached nearly to the ceiling. It supported heavy curtains that enclosed the bed. There was a practical reason for this. Since the rooms in a castle were very draughty, these curtains created a protected place where the lord and his family could sleep. Only the lord and his family had beds—although several children slept

together in the same bed. Everyone else in the castle slept on straw mattresses, even the guests. The guests' servants frequently slept on piles of straw in the stables.

Even during the day—especially in winter—castles were dark. On long winter evenings the lord's family and guests gathered around an open fireplace or stove. This gave off some light. There were also long pine splinters held in iron rings on the walls.

Was there any lighting?

The family and guests of the castle lord are gathered in the Knights' Hall. Sitting in front of the large fireplace they listen to a troubadour's song.

They gave off a little light as well. For festivals servants made torches by wrapping sticks in cloth soaked in tar or tree resin. Since the wooden floors and scattered straw caught fire so easily, people used pine splinters and torches as little as possible. The safest light was a small tallow lamp—a clay lamp filled with animal fat (tallow). This caused a lot of smoke, however, and also a strong smell.

fashions of the 12th century   fashions of the 13th century

In everyday life the clothing of the nobility was little different from that of the servants.

What did the castle residents wear?

Above all, their clothes had to be practical and to protect them from wind and weather. They all wore underwear made of coarse linen, and it was usually very scratchy. Over this they wore a second garment, a kind of long-sleeved undershirt that reached down to the knee for men and to the calf for women. It was tied at the waist with a rope or leather belt. Women wore stockings, and men wore tight-fitting pants that reached down to their ankles. In later times many noblemen began wearing two single pant legs. They were attached to the man's belt and were sometimes even of two different colors.

Over all of this came an overgarment. For poor people it was usually made of undyed wool, for the rich it was made of expensive and colorful fabrics. It was usually sleeveless. Noble men and women often added sleeves afterwards, attaching them with buttons or ribbons. The sleeves were usually a different color than the garment itself.

When it was cold, they wore a cloak that they could wrap around and fasten with a buckle. In winter people often wore leather clothing. The rich often had the insides of their overgarments lined with fur. The poor simply wore two overgarments on frosty days.

To protect themselves from the elements men and women wore hoods or leather caps while working.

What did they wear on their heads?

Married women and widows hid their hair under some kind of head covering, usually a wide bonnet. The hats of

DRESS CODE

In the early Middle Ages clothing was still quite simple, but it soon grew more and more colorful and exotic. Priests often preached against the extravagance of the nobles' clothing. When wealthier peasants and city dwellers began imitating the nobles' fashions, the nobles and the clergy saw this as a threat to the social order. As a result, during the 13th and 14th centuries the nobility issued dress codes. They strictly forbid commoners to wear the styles of nobles and restricted what craftsmen and servants could wear. Rules limited how colorful their clothes could be, and how much fur or ribbon they could use to adorn them.

fashions of the 14th century   *fashions of the 15th century*

CLOTHING AND FASHION

Until the 12th century castle dwellers all wore long-sleeved, sack-like garments. Class differences were seen only in the quality of materials used. Then people started adding pleats or slits to accentuate their figures. In the 14th century women added trains to their dresses. The 15th century emphasized the waist, and preferred slender outlines underscored by pointed toes on shoes.

castle ladies were especially elaborate. Among other things they wore a hat shaped like a long cone, with long veils hanging from the tip. Young girls, on the other hand, were allowed to wear their hair without covering, and usually decorated it only with a small circlet—a thin ornate band that circled their head. Otherwise the dress of children and adults was exactly the same except for size.

Simple people usually wore wooden shoes or sandals. They carved the shoes themselves on cold winter days. There were also leather sandals that were laced up around the ankle and tied just above it. To keep them from sinking into the mud on wet roads, they gave them wooden soles.

Over time shoe fashions among the nobles became more and more extravagant. They liked to wear pointed shoes with tips so long they had to be tied back.

What did their shoes look like?

At the beginning of the Middle Ages men and women dressed very much alike. Above all, their clothing had to be practical. The difference between the clothing of the poor and the rich was seen primarily in the materials they were made of. The nobility could afford to buy fabrics that didn't scratch as much, and also leathers and furs that offered good protection against rain and cold.

Did fashions sometimes change?

As time went by, however, people became more fashion conscious. Clothing was designed to emphasize the figure, and to bring color into the grayness of everyday life—especially the clothes worn at celebrations.

"Pease porridge hot, pease porridge cold, pease porridge in the pot, nine days old." This verse accurately describes the daily

What did castle residents eat?

diet in castles and monasteries in the Middle Ages. It was not at all like what we see in movies about knights; it was simple and monotonous. It consisted mostly of bread and porridge—particularly appropriate since most people had bad teeth. The most important foodstuff was grain. Potatoes, rice, and noodles hadn't been discovered or invented yet.

Castle residents ate once in late morning and again just after sundown. Over time the first meal developed into two: breakfast and midday meal. The main foods were always fresh or old bread—which they dipped in milk or wine—and oatmeal, pea porridge, or millet gruel. At night there might be one or two warm dishes.

The various grains had different uses. They usually made rye into a dark, slightly sour-tasting bread. The nobles preferred wheat bread —in some parts of Europe it was even called "nobles' bread." Oats that weren't cooked into oatmeal were used for horse feed. Barley was mostly used for brewing beer.

Eggs and milk were also important foodstuffs, especially because they were readily available. Both had more nutrients than gruel or porridge, and part of the milk—which usually spoiled quite quickly—could be made into a thick, hard cheese that kept well. In the castle the only ones who ate this "peasant's food" were the servants.

Fish added variety to the diet prepared in castle kitchens. This medieval woodcut shows fishermen catching fish with a net.

Even for the family of the lord of the castle meat was a holiday dish. In fenced off areas in the woods belong-

What kinds of meat did they eat?

ing to the castle peasants and servants raised pigs. They fed them acorns and other products found in the forest. All other domestic animals were only slaughtered after they couldn't be used for anything else. For this reason cows,

LENT

Already in the Middle Ages Christians fasted in the period before Easter and on Fridays. Since they weren't allowed to eat meat from warm-blooded animals when they fasted, fish—a cold-blooded animal— became the most important food during such times. In one legend, an abbot tried to escape the monotony of this diet by taking a freshly killed wild boar, sprinkling water on it, and saying: "I baptize you and give you the name Carp!"

A master huntsman goes out hunting with his stable boy, his dog, and his horse. He is hunting wild game that will be served to the family of the castle lord.

THE DISHES used in castles were simple clay jugs and bowls. Craftsmen later developed glazed pottery and also started making pewter dishes. People ate with a knife and a wooden spoon—guests usually brought their own—and there were no forks. When they couldn't get food with a knife and spoon they used their fingers. Several people ate from the same dish. They soaked up sauces with bread.

HERBS AND SPICES

The most important spice in the Middle Ages was salt—in part because they needed it for preserving many foods. It was so expensive that the lord or lady kept it locked up and rationed it out. Whenever possible, cooks used fresh herbs from the garden to season foods. They also had foreign spices, however, like saffron, cinnamon, poppy seed, cloves, and "Indian salt" (an early name for sugar in some parts of Europe).

sheep, goats, and chickens were usually very tough and had to be boiled before they were roasted.

This kind of meat was a fairly regular if infrequent item in the castle kitchen. Wild game, on the other hand, was unusual, even though hunting was a favorite pastime of the nobility. The animals they hunted included deer, mountain goats, wild boars, and bears. They also hunted smaller game such as foxes and badgers.

Fish and crabs were also plentiful in the lakes and rivers. During Lent—the fasting period before Easter—people made their frugal meals more interesting by setting out with a rod and net to catch fish. They bought ocean fish like salted herring or dried cod from the market of the next city or from traveling merchants.

What did they grow in the castle garden?

The lady of the castle regularly sent her maid-servants into the woods to gather berries, nuts, mushrooms, chestnuts, and wild herbs like young stinging nettle or cress. She gave particular attention to planting a kitchen garden inside the castle ward, however, and to planting a fruit orchard nearby. In the garden she grew vegetables such as peas, lentils, beans, and also all kinds of cabbage. She also grew beets, fennel, celery, and leeks. A small section of the garden was reserved for herbs meant for medicinal uses rather than for seasoning foods.

There were many vegetables that could be dried or preserved and kept through the winter. Apples and nuts also kept well in a cool storage room. Plums, cherries, and pears were dried whole or in pieces—if they didn't get eaten right away while they were fresh.

APRILIS

A well-tended garden was part of every castle, and provided fruits, vegetables, and herbs. If the castle was small, the garden was usually outside the walls. In larger castles it was in the castle ward.

The most important drinks were well or spring water and cow or goat milk. Since they knew that water could easily be contaminated, and that dirty water made them sick, people often preferred beer or wine. They even gave it to their children. During the brewing and pressing processes the water was boiled and this killed the disease-causing bacteria—even if they didn't know this at the time.

The cheapest drink was beer. Local wines were also inexpensive if you lived in a wine region. The wines in northern areas were very sour and people sweetened them with honey. Sometimes the maidservants crushed ginger, cloves, and cinnamon and wrapped them in cloth and put this bag in the wine. As it "steeped," the wine was flavored by the spices. This became known as "mulled" wine. Another popular drink—and a highly alcoholic one—was mead, a wine-like drink made from honey.

In summer and fall people made juice out of cherries, plums, apples, and pears. Here too they learned that fermented juices were safer.

The brewer boiled a mash made of malt and hops, and the women assisting him filtered out the hop solids and put the beer into barrels to cool.

At the center of every castle kitchen was an open-hearth fire. On the wall to the left and right of this were brackets holding a roasting spit. The fire could get so hot that the kitchen assistant had to protect himself with a shield while he turned the roasting spit.

Kitchen servants did the cooking in large kettles. These hung from metal arms that could be swung out over the fire and then back off it. There were also clay pots that could be set directly into the fire. Raised, enclosed stoves weren't developed until the late Middle Ages. They made it easier to boil and stew foods. These cooking methods were developed by the Romans, and knights fighting in the crusades learned them and brought them back to Europe.

On the walls next to the roasting spits were all kinds of kitchen utensils: sieves, ladles, and other such things. There were also shelves for dishes and pots and also for containers holding flour and grains, spices and oil, and vinegar. There was also a large table where chickens were plucked and gutted, meat was cut up, and vegetables were washed.

How did they preserve foods?

Even though they didn't have refrigerators or canned goods, people in the Middle Ages still had ways of keeping foods for longer periods of time. In the summer they dried or pickled vegetables like beans, peas, and mushrooms and they kept easily through the winter. Fruit could be dried, too, but it could also be preserved in honey. They preserved meat by smoking it or by curing it in salt. First they dried the meat and then covered it with a layer of salt. This process worked even better when the meat was packed in a salt-soaked cloth. Sometimes fruits and meat were layered in a barrel; the fruit juices soaked into the meat and preserved it.

The center of the castle kitchen was the hearth. There was a roasting spit above the hearth, and also several iron devices on which the cook could hang pots.

The biggest problem was keeping preserved foods dry and safe from rodents and insects. This was no problem for wine or for meats pickled in barrels. Other foods had to be stored in sealed clay pots or in chests kept on the ground floor if it wasn't too damp. If it was wet, they often built a storage building next to the palace. Otherwise they relied on cats to keep the mouse population in check.

In the Middle Ages the only schools were in monasteries.

Was there a school in the castle?

Noble families only sent a son or daughter to such a school if they wanted the son to become a priest or the daughter to become a nun. All other children learned primarily from looking over the shoulder of a parent and by helping parents with their work.

A child's position in society and its occupation were usually decided already at birth: a peasant's son knew that he could become a peasant and nothing else; the daughter of a castle servant would serve as a maidservant, and the son of a castle lord would become a knight. His sister would marry a nobleman of equal rank—unless she went into a convent. For the children of simple people, then, an education in their parents' work was enough. For the sons and daughters of noble parents some training by hired tutors or by friends of the family was necessary.

Until they were seven years old, all the lord's children remained in their mother's care. They were allowed to play and to run about. Then they had to face the serious side of life: they were treated like adults, they started a strict apprenticeship, and they had chores and duties they had to fulfill.

The children of noble families didn't usually learn to read and write. There was no such thing as an over-crowded classroom in those days.

How were knights trained?

As soon as a boy was seven years old he left his parents and went to serve another knight as a page. The parents hoped their son would learn to cope with the harshness of the adult world in this way. This kind of education emphasized practical skills. The page learned to ride and care for horses, to fence and wrestle, to fight with a lance, and to take care of weapons and armor. He also had to wait on his lord at the table, help him dress, and carry messages for him. At the same time he learned the manners of "courtly life" from his foster parents—respectable behavior and good morals, for example.

At the age of 14 he became a squire and started the actual training to become a knight. He now

COURTLY ROMANCES were the most popular reading material in the castle—along with the Bible, of course. These were stories of noble knights, their bold deeds and adventures, their conflicts and virtues, and of their love for a high lady. Their virtues became a model for proper or "courtly" behavior.

The **"ACCOLADE"** marked the end of a young man's training for knighthood. In this ceremony, the squire was made a knight. The person conveying this honor often did so by touching the shoulder of the new knight with the flat of a sword. The knight was then given a sword—a symbol of his obligation to defend the weak and to fight off enemies.

Embroidery, sewing, and singing were some of the skills included in a young noble-woman's education. The lady of the castle provided a good example.

Famous Women

Despite the fact that men controlled most aspects of the medieval world, some women still made a name for themselves. Christine de Pisan lived in France in the 15th century and was a famous writer. The German Hildegard von Bingen achieved fame for her poetry and music, and for her medical and scientific works.

accompanied his foster father to court and to tournaments. He often took part in battles and feuds, since one of his duties was to assist his knight in battle. He also watched over his foster father's shoulder when he took care of administrative duties or when he pronounced judgment in legal cases.

It was certainly considered desirable for a young man to learn the basics of reading, writing, and arithmetic, but it wasn't absolutely necessary. In general the monk or chaplain who taught the would-be knight only taught him enough so he could grasp the general sense of documents and could add and subtract on an abacus. This was all he needed in order to check administrative records and be sure he wasn't being cheated. It was more important that he learn other languages—writing and arithmetic could be left to a monk or scribe. Latin wasn't as important since it was only used in official docu-

ments, but being able to speak French—or for people living on the continent, to speak English—was important. During the crusades and in other European conflicts they had already seen how useful it was to be able to communicate with both friends and enemies.

A daughter of a noble family had a clear path in life: she was to marry a man of the proper social standing, have children, and be capable of managing the castle household. A girl was generally trained at home, and the most important teacher was her mother. She helped her mother with all of the daily work.

How were young girls educated?

Unmarried or widowed relatives taught her to spin, sew, and embroider. They used one of the heated rooms for these classes. In addition to practical skills, a young girl was taught to sing, play an instrument, and read aloud. Girls were often better educated than boys—girls could usually read and write. Many of them knew by heart the knightly legends written in verses. Since many of the popular knightly romances were in French and English, they might also learn a foreign language.

Once a girl reached marriageable age her parents might take her to live at a major court. Here her chances were better for finding a good match. Influential family friends often helped to negotiate a marriage. She could also learn social graces here by serving as a lady-in-waiting to the queen or duchess.

Puppet theater (book illumination).

What games did children play?

Our present-day distinction between work and leisure time was unknown to the residents of a castle. When there was work to do—and there almost always was—it began with the break of day and ended only when it became too dark to work anymore. Only Sundays and church holidays stood out from the everyday work routine. After church services and meals that might last for hours, there was time left for conversation and entertainment.

Smaller children had the whole day free to play. Using dolls made of clay or wood they imitated the world of their parents, as children still do today. They also played some games we still play today: blind man's bluff, jump rope, catch, and hide-and-seek. The castle was an ideal playground. The children also had toys we would recognize today: tops, pinwheels, hobbyhorses, and marbles.

In the winter children might go ice skating with the adults. Under shoes made out of wood they had blades made of animal bone and they used poles to move themselves forward. Boys often played at being knights and would take the pole under their arm and skate towards each other as if they were jousting.

What games or hobbies did adults have?

Among the games adults played were several board games. The most popular was trictrac, a game known today as backgammon. Chess, checkers, and other board games were played

This illumination shows two knights playing tric-trac, a game now known as backgammon.

In this illumination a knight plays chess with his wife. This was one of his favorite activities.

ITINERANT ENTERTAINERS

During long winter evenings, noble lords and ladies were happy to have itinerant (traveling) entertainers in the castle. They played instruments like the fiddle, harp, and viola da gamba, and sang songs about courtly love and knightly adventures. Many nobles played instruments themselves, wrote poetry, and also sang. Their castle became a social gathering place. Jugglers, bear trainers, and dancers were also welcome.

the castle ward or on a meadow outside the castle. Here two teams played with a ball made from a pig's bladder filled with dried peas. Using hands and feet they tried to move the ball across the playing field to one of two goals. This is one of the games that later developed into present-day soccer.

During winters the only things

What was the favorite pastime of knights?

people had to help fight boredom were board games or, for women, sewing. During the rest of the year, however, between battles and tournaments, nobles preferred hunting above all other leisure activities. Women and clergymen also participated in the hunt.

In the broad forests that existed in Europe during the Middle Ages, there were still many deer, wild boars, foxes, and bears. They were hunted with the same weapons the men used in battle: bow and arrow, spear, and crossbow. The most prized object of the hunt was the male wild boar. Because of its sharp tusks, it was considered more dangerous than an armed man.

For the kind of hunt where servants beat the bushes to drive wild game toward the hunters, most nobles owned special horses. They often treated them better than the servants who assisted on the hunt. Hunting dogs were also very important. They caught the scent of the game and then tracked it down. Falcons were also highly valued assistants. Through years of training they could learn to snare birds, rabbits, and hares.

The preferred hobby of most nobles was the hunt. Training falcons and then using them to hunt was especially popular. When the falcon killed an animal, it returned to its master, who put a hood over its head so it would calm down again.

in castles throughout Europe. Domino was played with tiles of wood or clay and existed in many variations. The church tried to suppress dice games, which were very popular among the nobility. In long winter nights many a horse or piece of land was lost to dice.

When weather permitted, castle residents met with people from a neighboring village for games in

Attacking and Defending the Castle

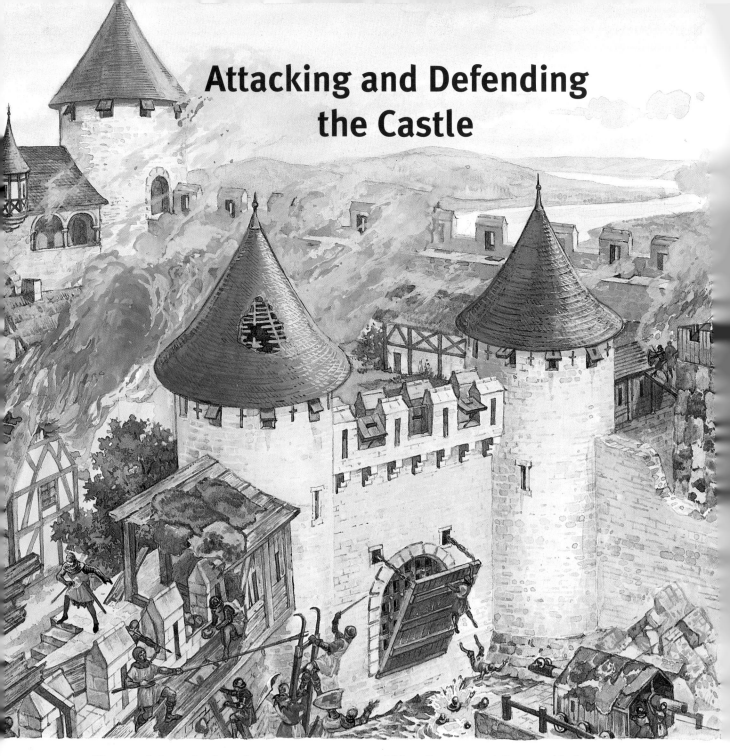

What were the castle's most important defensive structures?

The castle's main function was to shield against attacks by robber bands or hostile armies. Europe's nobles were quick to start feuds and the aim of their attacks was always their enemy's center of power, his castle. The defenders hoped the enemy would be discouraged from attacking just by the sight of the mighty walls and towers. The castle site had been chosen because it could be defended easily. The building itself was designed so that it would be hard if not impossible to penetrate into the interior of the castle.

The most important defensive structure was the wall surrounding

Attackers concentrated on the weakest points in the castle. They tried to break down the castle gate with a battering ram. With burning arrows they set roofs on fire. Only after the castle defenses were worn down by such tactics did the enemy push the siege tower up to the walls.

The **PORTCULLIS** consisted of wooden or iron beams that tapered to a point at the bottom. It hung by ropes or chains. Watchmen and soldiers used a winch above the door to raise or lower the portcullis. Behind the portcullis were two heavy doors that could be secured with a heavy beam that was stored in a slot in the side wall. Behind the gate there was often a deep ditch that had been dug to create one more obstacle for any attackers who made it this far.

The front end of a battering ram was often given the shape of a ram's head.

the castle. It was particularly thick and strong at points where the enemy could get right up to the wall without facing steep slopes or deep water. There were small, wedge-shaped slits in the castle wall—arrow loops—that got wider towards the inside. This allowed archers to move and take aim, but still offered them good protection.

On top of the wall, running along its length, was the walk. It was protected by the battlement, a wall that ran along the outside of the walk. The battlement had high parts called merlons, and low parts called embrasures. Archers and soldiers with small catapults could take cover behind the merlons in between shots through the embrasures. Parts of the walk protruded out over the edge of the wall. There were holes in the floor of these parts and defenders could drop rocks, hot oil, or smelly manure through these holes onto the attackers below.

Rounded towers jutted out from the castle wall. From these towers soldiers could see even the base of the walls and could shoot at any enemy who had made it up to the wall.

Larger castles had an inner wall or "curtain" that encircled the palace and inner ward, and an outer wall or "curtain" that enclosed the outer ward. Often both walls had deep moats dug in front of them. An enemy had to pass through this heavily guarded inner ward to reach the palace itself.

What protected the entrance to the castle?

The weak point in every castle was the gate, since it had to be wide enough to allow horses and wagons into the castle ward. In times of war it was the first site attackers focused on. There was usually a water-filled moat between the gate and the road leading up to it. The gate could only be reached by crossing a drawbridge. When soldiers needed to defend the gatehouse, they could release the drawbridge and it

This illumination shows the storming of a castle. The mounted knights are trying to attack the lowered portcullis.

swung upward, breaking off access to the gate. In times of danger the drawbridge was often left up permanently. To enter the castle you had to cross a narrow bridge and go up a narrow stairway that allowed only one person at a time into the castle.

The next obstacle was a heavy gate that could be dropped into place—the portcullis. Guards could quickly lower it to block the gate.

How did the enemy attack the castle?

Capturing the castle was difficult and complicated. Since the attacking army knew this, they often attempted to take the castle by surprise. This tactic was usually only successful when the enemy had managed to bribe several men inside the castle so that they wouldn't report the approach of the enemy troops, or so that they would leave the gates open and unguarded.

If the castle couldn't be taken quickly, the enemy besieged it. They tried to starve the defenders so they would have to give up. First the enemy surrounded the castle, set the surrounding farms on fire, and cut off supply roads. Then they scouted out the area to see how they could best get their siege machinery up to the castle. With castles in high places this was especially difficult. As soon as one of the oxen carts transporting parts of the war machine started up the steep, winding road, it was showered with a hail of arrows.

SECRET PASSAGES are more common in legend than in reality. In the Middle Ages workers could only build such passages if the ground under the castle wasn't too rocky to dig into. Where they did exist, they led out into the open at a place as hidden as possible.

Underground rooms with hidden doors, on the other hand, were common. They served as hiding places for people and possessions.

The moats posed a further obstacle. They first had to be filled with earth, branches, and stones before the siege machines could be pushed up to the castle. The enemy usually tried to do this during the night, since the defenders otherwise threw stones down on them or poured hot tar over them.

What weapons were used during a siege?

First, the enemy rolled a low wooden shed up to the gate or one of the walls. Using chains, they suspended a massive log from one of the shed's roof beams. The log had a metal cap at the front end. Often this cap was shaped like a ram's head. The roof of the battering "ram" was covered with wet animal skins to protect it from burning arrows. Soldiers swung the log back and forth and tried to ram in the gates or a part of the wall in this way.

At the same time other soldiers set up large catapults in front of the castle walls. At the back end of such a machine there was a winch that the soldiers used to pull the throwing arm downward. When the soldiers let go of the rope the catapult arm shot up into the air since there was a heavy weight at the other end. This machine was used to catapult stones over the walls into the defending forces. Sometimes it was used to catapult other objects such as manure, dead animals, or clay jars filled with stinking substances into

Soldiers used a heavy winch to pull the catapult arm back. A catapult could pelt walls and towers with stones or other missiles weighing hundreds of pounds.

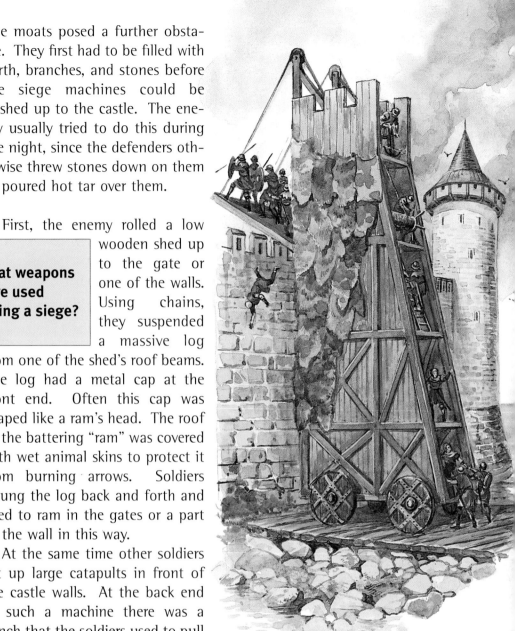

After the castle moat had been filled in and perhaps leveled with boards, soldiers rolled the siege tower up to the wall.

the castle. The soldiers operating the machine protected themselves from the defender's arrows by setting up large wooden shields. Occasionally the besieging forces also tried to catapult fire pots into the castle. These fire pots contained a mixture of sulfur, resin, tar, oil, and cooking salt. Once this mixture was ignited, it was very difficult to extinguish the fire. The besieged forces had to work hard to put out such fires.

If the ground around the castle was suitable, the besieging forces tried to dig a tunnel under the castle walls. This could take weeks of work. The tunnel was supported by wooden beams. Once the foundations of the wall had been un-

The enemy troops usually had a number of siege weapons. They tried to do the most possible damage with these weapons.

dercut, the diggers set the wooden supports on fire and hoped that when the tunnel collapsed the wall above would collapse as well.

What happened when the enemy stormed the castle?

Besieging a castle was an attempt to weaken the walls, nerves, and energies of the defenders, and it took weeks or even months. When the enemy forces thought the defenders and the castle were weakened enough, they might decide to storm the castle at dawn, using all their forces at once. They set the underground tunnels on fire, pushed battering rams up to the walls at several points, kept a constant fire of catapult missiles flying into the castle, and their archers attempted to shoot down any sol-

dier that tried to move along the walk at the top of the walls.

Now the siege towers were brought into the battle. It took a long time to build them, they were very expensive and could easily be damaged by catapult missiles or set on fire by burning arrows. As a result, they were usually kept in reserve until the last moment. These huge, heavy towers had to be taller than the walk along the castle's walls. As archers on top of the tower shot at the soldiers on the wall, soldiers on the next level lowered a drawbridge onto the wall and attempted to rush over onto the castle walk. At the same time the other forces doubled their efforts so that defenders couldn't concentrate on the siege tower alone.

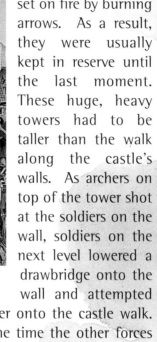

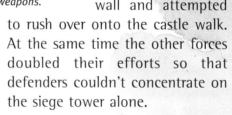

If the siege tower made it to the wall, attacking forces could climb up its back side and cross over a drawbridge and get onto the castle wall. Here some of the most bitter fighting took place.

A castle had to be ready for a

How did the castle residents prepare for a siege?

siege at any time. The enemy's goal was to starve the castle inhabitants so there would be as little resistance as possible when they stormed the walls. The most important preparation therefore was securing food and water supplies. They stored as much grain and other staples as they possibly could. They also replenished these supplies constantly since they were perishable. If the defenders could build up a large enough supply before enemy forces arrived, they had already won half the battle.

Carpenters built temporary wooden barriers that extended out from the battlements and towers. These barriers were called "hoardings." They were designed so they could be set up or taken down quickly. To protect them from fire soldiers put wet animal skins over them and sprayed the skins regularly to keep them wet. From the hoardings soldiers could drop rocks or tar on the enemy below.

The soldiers also had to maintain and assemble the catapults and make sure they had plenty of tar, rocks, and arrows on hand.

In general there were no more

How did they defend the castle?

than 30 armed men in a medium-sized castle. Their opponents were often several hundred in number. Even when the defenders succeeded in stopping the enemy's greater forces with their rocks and arrows, and in repulsing attack

after attack, they were still trapped in the castle. The morale of the soldiers was an important factor on both sides and each side tried to undermine the other.

It was particularly demoralizing for the defenders that long stretches of deceptive quiet might pass and then day after day of stones flying over the walls, and

After weeks or even months of siege conditions it wasn't unusual for both sides to agree to negotiate. Often this led to a solution that allowed both sides to save face.

finally a sudden attack. The defenders couldn't tell whether the attack was real or only a trick. Within the castle walls they could not do much other than throw obstacles on the soldiers storming the walls. In rare cases they might leave the castle for brief attacks to try and destroy one of the siege machines.

To find out if the enemy was digging tunnels under the walls, soldiers placed bowls of water in the castle basement. If ripples appeared in the water, danger was near. Then the watch tried to see from one of the towers where the enemy was digging. The defending soldiers then provided additional support for the wall where the tunnel threatened.

How long did a siege last?

It was rare that a siege lasted longer than a year. If they succeeded in taking the castle before the defenders surrendered, the besieging forces probably showed little mercy. Usually the fight was decided much earlier, however. When food supplies became short or enemy forces were too great, when no help was in sight or the castle inhabitants

There were many castles that survived for several centuries without being attacked even once. This was probably because they created the impression of being impossible to capture.

became sick, the result was often a negotiated surrender. An unconditional surrender was uncommon. The victor let the conquered lord preserve his honor and even part of his possessions. Often he made an ally of the defeated lord through treaties. If the attackers saw that the defending forces could hold out for a long time, they often withdrew, usually before winter could cause more casualties than a direct attack on the castle would.

A Celebration at the Castle

Life in a castle was hard and its inhabitants did without many things. Everyone looked forward to the celebrations that interrupted the monotony of everyday life. At the beginning of spring, after the harvest, or on a church holiday, the lord invited his subjects to a free meal with free drinking, dancing, and entertainment.

What occasions did they celebrate?

On special occasions he held great festival celebrations that could last for days. The lord and lady invited guests from near and far, and merchants and singers, jugglers and other traveling entertainers came to provide entertainment. Since a festival like this cost a lot of money and used up a lot of food, the castle lord couldn't afford to hold one very often. Usually his father's funeral was the first major celebration to which he invited guests. This was also his first appearance as the new lord, and he wanted to show himself in the best light to his peers and his subjects.

He also held major celebrations for important family events such as engagements, marriages, or baptisms. In many cases parents arranged a daughter's engagement while she was still in the cradle. Other occasions calling for celebration were the safe return of soldiers from the crusades, the acquisition of a new title and new land, or the day the lord's heir was dubbed a knight. On such days the ruler of the land usually came to the castle as well.

How did the lord and lady prepare for the festivities?

A major celebration required months of preparations. First messengers rode out with the invitations and noted how many accepted and how many declined

Pages carry a "course for the eyes" up to the high table, where the lord and his guests are seated. Musicians and perhaps a court jester would provide entertainment.

FESTIVAL DINNERS started early in the day. They usually began around 11 or 12 o'clock and lasted several hours.

the invitations. Then the lady of the castle made an exact list of the supplies the peasants would need to provide and of the items she would have to buy in the city. At the same time she engaged well-known

singers and other artists who could provide for elegant entertainment. The castle lord might invite a prominent preacher for church services during the celebration, and heralds for a tournament. The castle was given a major cleaning and the floors were strewn with fresh reeds and straw.

At every court festival musicians played music for dancing (book illumination).

The celebration began—these

What took place during a major celebration?

were very religious times—with a religious service in the morning. The priest looked down from the pulpit at his elegantly dressed listeners and this gave him the topic for his sermon: luxury and gluttony were spreading and the god-fearing way of life was going out of style! Dozens of sermons like this have been preserved, but the listeners don't seem to have taken them very seriously.

The castle and the surrounding area had been turned into one large festival site. The main attraction was usually a tournament. In the beginning a tournament meant athletic contests in which hundreds of men met to test their fighting skills as if in battle. In the course of the 13th century this developed into an event where knights could demonstrate their skill in handling both horses and weapons. In one-on-one competition two opponents galloped toward each other and each tried to unseat the other with his lance. The victor was the one who remained seated. In these tournaments the competitors were often "professionals," that is, knights who went from tournament to tournament and earned their living from the prizes.

Surrounding the tournament grounds were dozens of attractions. The news of a celebration spread quickly among itinerant (traveling) entertainers and many of them hurried to the castle. On the day of the celebration there were tightrope walkers, jugglers performing tricks, and a veiled woman told the future—much to

TABLE MANNERS

We know that people didn't always show good manners at festival dinners from the many etiquette books that have survived. "Don't spit on the table," it says in one of them. Or: "Wipe your mouth before you drink" (since several people shared the same goblet). People were instructed not to belch, not to pick their teeth, and not to put bones back onto the serving plate but rather into a container for bones that was kept under the table.

At the center of every festival was the tournament. Before the actual jousting began, the knights demonstrated their riding skills.

SILVERWARE was unknown. People either ate with their fingers or skewered things with a knife. It was considered polite to offer your neighbor at the table small bites of food. Forks weren't introduced until the late Middle Ages.

the chagrin of the priest. A bear keeper led his animal in dances, and a puppeteer made his marionettes perform the story of a knight fighting the heathens in the Holy Land. A singer or troubadour performed a song making fun of a neighbor the castle lord didn't like and was given a handsome tip as a reward.

In one of the most popular variants of jousting a knight tried to lift his opponent out of his saddle with a lance.

Scores of beggars found their way into the castle. They could be sure that even the stingy nobles would be more generous on such a day. Maidservants distributed fresh bread and dried fruit to the guests, and the smell of an ox roasting on a spit filled the air.

Late in the afternoon pages called all the guests into the Knights' Hall. It was now decorated with garlands of greenery and flowers and with bright flags. The guests of honor sat together with the lord of the castle and his wife at the head of the hall on high-backed chairs behind a long table on a raised platform—the "high table." The other guests sat on benches at tables along the long sides of the hall. The entourage—the lesser figures at court—sat on the benches in niches along the walls. As a rule, the "high table" received one half of all the food, the other guests got one fourth, and all the others in the benches along the walls had to share the remaining quarter. They were given the smaller rolls and the pastries filled with organ meat from the animals whose filets had been given to the more noble guests.

The dinner consisted of several courses, each of which were made up of four or five dishes. The foods were carried in on silver and gold trays by pages and kitchen servants. They started with salads and soups. For example, there was a pea soup made of cooked and pureed peas with bacon and milk, with cooked pork mixed in. A "cinnamon bouillon" was made of hens cooked in water and wine, served with a thick cinnamon sauce.

After the appetizers a course of wild game was served. This included roasted leg of venison, swan and heron pieces baked in a crust, or rabbit in ginger sauce.

> **What did they eat at the festival dinner?**

For the main course there was dove in pastry shells, roasted leg of mutton, baked carp, or partridge in sorrel sauce.

The finale included apple or pear slices, grapes, toasted white bread, and as a climax, "sweetmeats." These were exotic, candied fruits such as oranges, dates, and figs, but also local fruits such as fennel, ginger, juniper berries, and nuts that were heavily sugared.

There was often also a course for the eyes, one meant to be seen more than eaten. A popular dish of this sort was an eagle that was put back into its coat of feathers after it was cooked. The cook then pushed thin iron rods into the bird so that it stood upright on the platter with its wings spread wide. Finally a clump of wool saturated in camphor was placed in its mouth and then lit on fire so that the eagle entered the hall "spewing fire."

Meat and vegetables were served cut into small pieces since people ate with their hands—forks were unknown at that time. Very hot pieces of meat were skewered with a knife and held up to the mouth. Usually only the "high table" had plates. The other guests used a slice of bread for a plate. After the meal the bread "plates" were given to the beggars at the gates.

Between courses famous and well paid singers performed.

How did they entertain their guests?

These troubadours, who usually came from the south of France and were often singer, poet, and knight all in one, per-

formed songs that were generally about courtly love. Courtly love was the passionate devotion to a woman who was usually already married and thus unattainable for the knight who worshiped her. He performed heroic deeds for her, won victories at tournaments, and even did nonsensical things like drinking her bath water. Of course this kind of admiration occurred in songs more so than in reality.

At the high point of the evening one or more of the singers sang parts of one of the great heroic legends. In England and on the continent they sang of King Arthur and his round table, in France of

We are reminded of the Middle Ages today by castles and churches, statues and paintings—and countless book illustrations or miniatures. A book with such illustrations is called an "illuminated manuscript." They show life as the artists of that time saw it.

Poets and singers were highly respected figures at the castle. This illumination shows a singer receiving a wreath of honor from the lady of the castle.

46

COAT-OF-ARMS

So friend and foe could recognize them in the heat of battle or in a tournament, knights needed a personal symbol—their "coat-of-arms." At first this was only a small flag on the end of their lances. Starting in the 13th century these symbols were painted onto the knight's shield or weapons. This is why a coat-of-arms is often shaped like a shield. It wasn't long until it was also carved above the castle entrance and became the family's personal symbol. Since a coat-of-arms was passed on from father to son, we can tell from it what family a person comes from.

Neuschwanstein Castle in Southern Germany isn't a medieval castle at all, but rather a "fairytale castle" built in the 19th century by Ludwig the Second, king of Bavaria.

Roland and Charlemagne, in Germany of the Nibelungs, for example. These heroic legends were also meant to teach a lesson, since they showed how a true knight should behave. Sometimes the singers wove current events into the story—often at the request of the host.

When the last dishes had been taken away, musicians came and played dance music. The lords and ladies lined up and began to move toward each other in measured steps. In the course of the evening the dances became more and more lively, and the noble couples spun about as wildly as the simple people did. The celebration continued until the early morning hours.

Were castles still used after the Middle Ages?

With the rise of rifles and cannons the age of castles came to an end. Even the thickest of walls couldn't protect against cannon balls. The kings and rulers of this new age—the Renaissance—built more splendid palaces and the castles fell into disrepair. During various rebellions of peasants and other commoners during the next centuries many castles were destroyed since they symbolized the oppression of the peasants by the nobility. Only a few noble families managed to preserve their castles as actual residences.

It wasn't until the 19th century that castles came into fashion again. The rising middle class tried to become "nobility" by buying old castles and restoring them as homes. At the same time legends of medieval knights and heroes were rediscovered and provided plots for operas, plays, and novels.

Today people are trying to preserve the few remaining castles. Most private owners can't afford to keep up a castle on their own—even if they are rich—and so governments give them support. The majority of castles are maintained by the governments of the countries where they are found. To recover the high costs of caring for castles, governments make them into tourist attractions. There are many castles you can visit today. Others have been made into hotels, museums, restaurants, or schools, and thus make a fascinating part of the past serve both pleasurable and practical functions.

Glossary

Arrow loop a vertical or cross-shaped slit in the castle wall through which archers could shoot their arrows.

Battering ram a large beam or log suspended from a moveable framework and used for ramming in walls or the doors of a castle gate.

Battlement a narrow, chest-high wall built along the outside of the walk at the top of the castle wall, usually with alternating *merlons* and *embrasures*.

Castellum a Roman fortified camp, model for later European castles—and the source of the word "castle."

Castle chaplain the priest who held services in the castle chapel.

Catapult machine that hurled stones or other missiles into a castle under siege.

Cesspit pit underneath the castle walls into which excrement from an interior *garderobe* fell.

Cistern container in which rainwater was collected and stored. Pipes running from the cistern supplied the castle with water.

Coat-of-arms the symbol on a knight's shield or suit of armor by which he was recognized. It later became the hereditary symbol of the family and its castle.

Courtly love devotion to a lady of higher rank, usually one already married.

Crossbow a bow mounted horizontally on a wooden stock (like a gunstock) and fired by pulling a trigger. It fired an arrow with greater force than a regular bow.

Crusades series of wars fought by Christian knights in the *Middle Ages* to free the Holy Land from "heathens" (non-Christians).

Curtain strong wall surrounding a castle *ward*. Often there was an inner curtain and an outer curtain.

Drawbridge bridge that led across the moat and could be pulled up to cut off access to the castle.

Embrasure the open spaces in the battlement—between the *merlons*—through which archers shot arrows or soldiers dropped rocks or other missiles.

Feudalism medieval societal order in which a *liege lord* (a king, for example) rules his lands by granting subjects temporary control over border lands as a reward for faithful service. In return the *liegeman* must protect the lands (the *fief*) from invaders and come to the aid of the king if he is attacked. The new lord becomes the ruler over all peasants and freemen living in the lands he now controls.

Fief land granted temporarily by a *liege lord* to a subordinate. In return the *liegeman* is obligated to serve the liege lord whenever needed and to provide troops for him in times of war.

Garderobe a toilet either built into an internal wall of a castle or jutting out from an outside wall.

Great Hall also called Knights' Hall. A room where guests were received and festival dinners were held.

Half-timber construction method in which the walls are built of a framework of heavy beams and the spaces between the beams are filled in with wattle (a grid of willow twigs) and daub (a mixture of clay or mud and straw, hair, etc.).

Itinerant entertainers singers or musicians who don't live in a fixed place but move from castle to castle to find work.

Liege lord an emperor, king, duke, or knight who grants some of his land to a *liegeman* as a *fief*.

Liegeman someone who has been given a *fief*.

Master builder a very skilled builder and engineer who had proven himself on many jobs and now ran building projects on his own, overseeing every part of the project and hiring the other craftsmen.

Merlon the raised part of the *battlement* behind which a soldier or archer could take cover.

Middle Ages historical period between the ancient world of the Greeks and Romans and the modern rebirth or "Renaissance" of that ancient culture. Usually identified as the period between the 5th and 16th centuries and divided into the Early (5th to 9th/11th centuries), High (9th/11th to 13th/14th centuries), and Late Middle Ages (13th/14th to 16th centuries).

Motte earliest form of the castle. A tower built on an artificial hill and surrounded by a *palisade*. The owner lived in the tower.

Page boy from a noble family, 7 to 14 years old, who was training to become a knight.

Palace main building of a medieval castle, containing the rooms in which the lord and his family lived, and also the *Great Hall*.

Palisade a sturdy wall made of sharply pointed logs rammed into the ground close together.

Portcullis heavy grille of wooden beams positioned between the two towers of the castle gate. It could be raised or lowered to close the passage through the gate.

Putlog hole a hole left in the masonry of a wall so that a scaffolding beam could be inserted.

Siege tower a wooden tower on wheels, used to get soldiers onto the wall of the castle they are besieging.

Squire young nobleman 14 years of age or older, who is continuing his training to become a knight by serving a nobleman who is already a knight.

Stone mason craftsman who cuts and finishes stones.

Tournament a medieval competition in which knights tested themselves against other knights in battle skills.

Troubadour a French term for a medieval singer who wrote and performed songs that centered on the ideal of *courtly love*.

Vassal another word for *liegeman*.

Walk the walkway running along the top of the castle wall or *curtain*. It was usually protected toward the outside by a *battlement*.

Ward yard inside the wall or *curtain* of a castle. Where there were two curtains it resulted in an inner and an outer ward.